About Skill Builders Fractions, Decimals, & Percents

by R. B. Snow and Clareen Arnold

Welcome to RBP Books' Skill Builders series. Like our Summer Bridge Activities collection, the Skill Builders series is designed to make learning both fun and rewarding.

Skill Builders Fractions, Decimals, & Percents introduces students to beginning concepts to help them reinforce and develop math skills. Each Skill Builders volume is grade-level appropriate, with clear examples and instructions to guide the lesson. In accordance with NCTM standards, exercises for Fractions, Decimals, & Percents cover a variety of math skills, including identifying fractions, mixed numbers, simplifying and renaming fractions, adding and subtracting fractions, multiplying fractions, converting fractions and decimals, standard operations with decimals, and more.

A critical thinking section includes exercises to develop higher-order thinking skills.

Learning is more effective when approached with an element of fun and enthusiasm—just as most children approach life. That's why the Skill Builders combine entertaining and academically sound exercises and fun themes to make reviewing basic skills fun and effective, for both you and your budding scholars.

Table of Contents

Identifying Fractions

A fraction tells about equal parts of a whole. The top number, called the **numerator**, tells how many parts are shaded. The bottom number, called the **denominator**, tells how many parts in all.

numerator ⟶ $\dfrac{1}{6}$
denominator ⟶

Write the correct fraction.

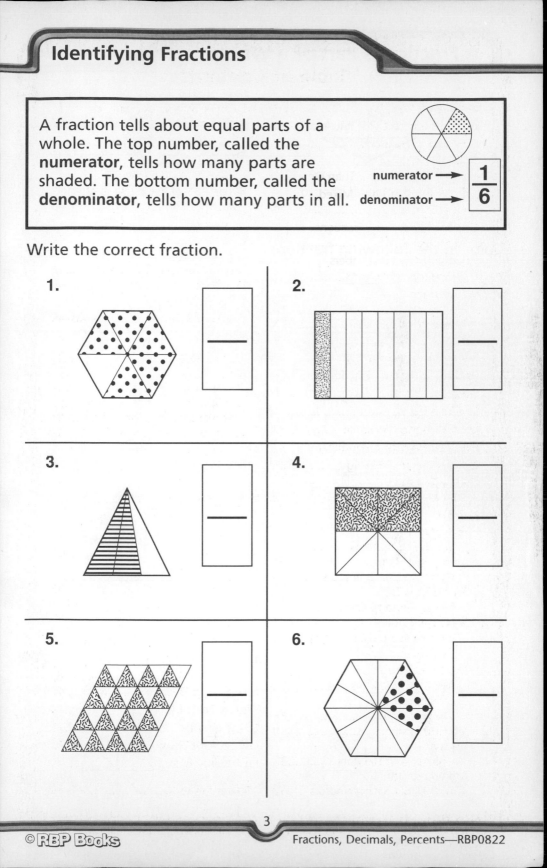

1.

2.

3.

4.

5.

6.

Fractions, Decimals, Percents—RBP0822

A Fraction Is Part of a Whole

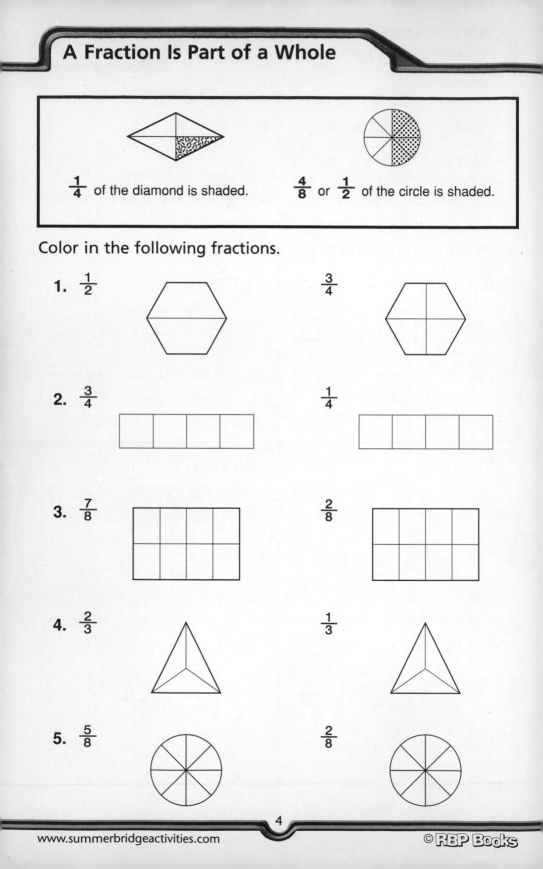

$\frac{1}{4}$ of the diamond is shaded. $\frac{4}{8}$ or $\frac{1}{2}$ of the circle is shaded.

Color in the following fractions.

1. $\frac{1}{2}$ $\frac{3}{4}$

2. $\frac{3}{4}$ $\frac{1}{4}$

3. $\frac{7}{8}$ $\frac{2}{8}$

4. $\frac{2}{3}$ $\frac{1}{3}$

5. $\frac{5}{8}$ $\frac{2}{8}$

A Fraction Is Part of a Whole

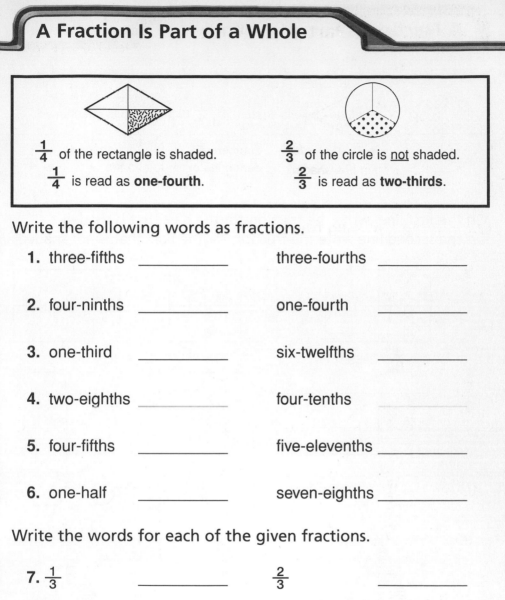

$\frac{1}{4}$ of the rectangle is shaded.

$\frac{1}{4}$ is read as **one-fourth**.

$\frac{2}{3}$ of the circle is <u>not</u> shaded.

$\frac{2}{3}$ is read as **two-thirds**.

Write the following words as fractions.

1. three-fifths _____   three-fourths _____

2. four-ninths _____   one-fourth _____

3. one-third _____   six-twelfths _____

4. two-eighths _____   four-tenths _____

5. four-fifths _____   five-elevenths _____

6. one-half _____   seven-eighths _____

Write the words for each of the given fractions.

7. $\frac{1}{3}$ _____ $\frac{2}{3}$ _____

8. $\frac{1}{2}$ _____ $\frac{1}{8}$ _____

9. $\frac{3}{8}$ _____ $\frac{4}{11}$ _____

10. $\frac{2}{5}$ _____ $\frac{5}{3}$ _____

11. $\frac{5}{7}$ _____ $\frac{5}{9}$ _____

5

A Fraction Is Part of a Whole

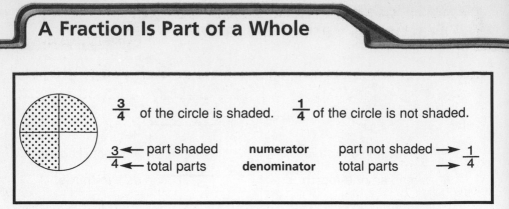

$\frac{3}{4}$ of the circle is shaded. $\frac{1}{4}$ of the circle is not shaded.

$\frac{3}{4}$ ← part shaded / total parts   **numerator** / **denominator**   part not shaded → total parts → $\frac{1}{4}$

On the first line, write the fraction for the part that is shaded.
On the second line write the fraction for the part that is not shaded.

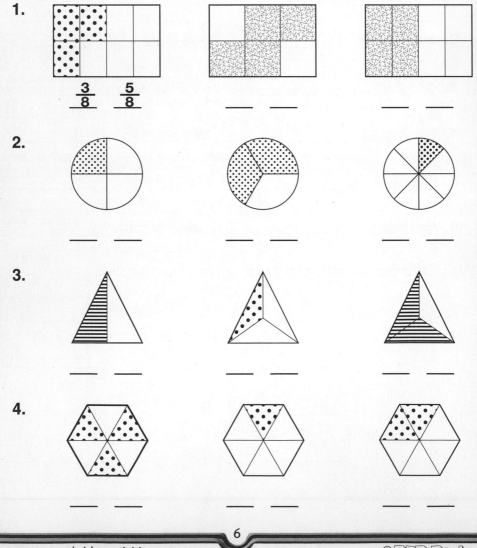

1. $\frac{3}{8}$ $\frac{5}{8}$ _____ _____   _____ _____

2.   _____ _____   _____ _____   _____ _____

3.   _____ _____   _____ _____   _____ _____

4.   _____ _____   _____ _____   _____ _____

6

Simplifying Mixed Numbers

$$2 \frac{20}{15} = 2 + \frac{20}{15}$$
$$= 2 + \frac{20 \div 5}{15 \div 5}$$
$$= 2 + \frac{4}{3}$$
$$= 3 \frac{1}{3}$$

When simplifying mixed numbers, simplify the fraction.

Simplify.

1. $\quad 2 \frac{2}{4}$ $\qquad\qquad 3 \frac{5}{15}$ $\qquad\qquad 2 \frac{12}{16}$

2. $\quad 1 \frac{6}{9}$ $\qquad\qquad 2 \frac{9}{2}$ $\qquad\qquad 6 \frac{3}{3}$

3. $\quad 2 \frac{5}{20}$ $\qquad\qquad 4 \frac{7}{21}$ $\qquad\qquad 5 \frac{9}{6}$

4. $\quad 4 \frac{9}{3}$ $\qquad\qquad 5 \frac{3}{12}$ $\qquad\qquad 2 \frac{3}{2}$

Simplify.

1. $\frac{6}{18}$ $\frac{12}{18}$ $\frac{20}{24}$

2. $\frac{18}{24}$ $\frac{9}{54}$ $\frac{6}{12}$

Write each of the following as a mixed number in simplest form.

3. $\frac{9}{8}$ $\frac{11}{5}$ $\frac{16}{6}$

4. $\frac{16}{3}$ $\frac{24}{16}$ $\frac{18}{4}$

5. $1\frac{5}{15}$ $2\frac{4}{6}$ $4\frac{3}{12}$

Renaming Fractions

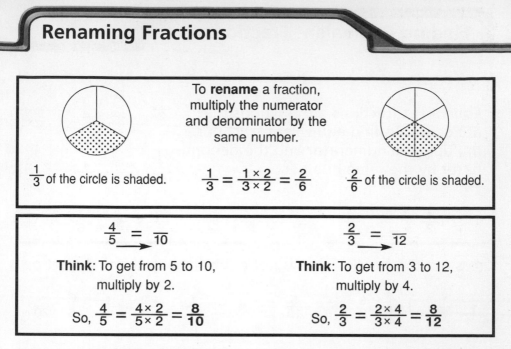

To **rename** a fraction, multiply the numerator and denominator by the same number.

$\frac{1}{3}$ of the circle is shaded.

$$\frac{1}{3} = \frac{1 \times 2}{3 \times 2} = \frac{2}{6}$$

$\frac{2}{6}$ of the circle is shaded.

$$\frac{4}{5} = \overline{10}$$

Think: To get from 5 to 10, multiply by 2.

So, $\frac{4}{5} = \frac{4 \times 2}{5 \times 2} = \frac{8}{10}$

$$\frac{2}{3} = \overline{12}$$

Think: To get from 3 to 12, multiply by 4.

So, $\frac{2}{3} = \frac{2 \times 4}{3 \times 4} = \frac{8}{12}$

Rename the following fractions using the denominator given.

1. $\frac{3}{4} = \overline{12}$ $\frac{4}{5} = \overline{15}$ $\frac{2}{3} = \overline{6}$

2. $\frac{1}{4} = \overline{16}$ $\frac{5}{6} = \overline{18}$ $\frac{3}{5} = \overline{20}$

3. $\frac{5}{8} = \overline{24}$ $\frac{2}{7} = \overline{14}$ $\frac{5}{6} = \overline{12}$

15

Finding Equivalent Fractions

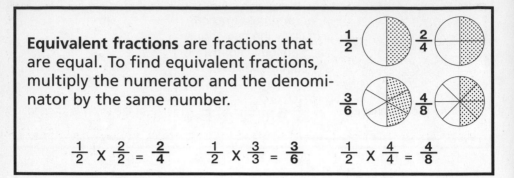

Equivalent fractions are fractions that are equal. To find equivalent fractions, multiply the numerator and the denominator by the same number.

$\frac{1}{2} \times \frac{2}{2} = \frac{2}{4}$ $\frac{1}{2} \times \frac{3}{3} = \frac{3}{6}$ $\frac{1}{2} \times \frac{4}{4} = \frac{4}{8}$

Cross out the fraction that is not equivalent to the first fraction.

1. $\frac{1}{3}$ = $\frac{2}{6}$ $\frac{3}{9}$ $\frac{4}{8}$ $\frac{5}{15}$

2. $\frac{1}{4}$ = $\frac{2}{8}$ $\frac{3}{6}$ $\frac{4}{16}$ $\frac{5}{20}$

3. $\frac{1}{5}$ = $\frac{2}{6}$ $\frac{2}{10}$ $\frac{3}{15}$ $\frac{4}{20}$

4. $\frac{2}{3}$ = $\frac{4}{6}$ $\frac{6}{9}$ $\frac{8}{16}$ $\frac{10}{15}$

Fill in the missing number.

5. $\frac{1}{4}$ = $\frac{3}{\boxed{}}$

6. $\frac{2}{\boxed{}}$ = $\frac{4}{6}$

7. $\frac{5}{8}$ = $\frac{\boxed{}}{16}$

8. $\frac{3}{4}$ = $\frac{9}{\boxed{}}$

9. $\frac{\boxed{}}{6}$ = $\frac{2}{12}$

10. $\frac{2}{3}$ = $\frac{\boxed{}}{9}$

Greatest Common Factor

Example: List the factors of 12 and 18.
Circle the common factors. Write the
greatest common factor (GCF).
Factors of 12: (1)(2)(3) 4,(6) 12
Factors of 18: (1)(2)(3)(6) 9, 18
Common Factors: (1)(2)(3)(6)   **GCF=6**

A **factor** is a number
that another
number can be
divided by evenly.

List the factors of each pair of numbers. Circle the common
factors. Find the greatest common factor (GCF).

1. 6:

18:

GCF:_____

4:

12:

GCF:_____

2. 12:

18:

GCF:_____

14:

21:

GCF:_____

3. 18:

27:

GCF:_____

24:

32:

GCF:_____

4. 9:

12:

GCF:_____

9:

15:

GCF:_____

5. 15:

20:

GCF:_____

15:

40:

GCF:_____

Simplest Form

Example: Write the fraction $\frac{42}{56}$ in simplest form.

Step 1
Find the GCF of the numerator and denominator.
42: ①②3, 6,⑦⑭㉑, ㊷
56: ①②4,⑦8, ⑭ 28, 56
GCF = 14

Step 2
Divide the numerator and denominator by their GCF.

$\frac{42}{56} \div \frac{14}{14} = \frac{3}{4}$

Write each fraction in simplest form. Circle your answer.
If a fraction is already in simplest form, just write the fraction.

1. $\frac{4}{6}$ $\frac{5}{10}$ $\frac{9}{15}$

2. $\frac{3}{27}$ $\frac{5}{18}$ $\frac{15}{18}$

3. $\frac{6}{21}$ $\frac{28}{42}$ $\frac{22}{30}$

4. $\frac{7}{21}$ $\frac{19}{38}$ $\frac{48}{60}$

5. $\frac{34}{59}$ $\frac{22}{88}$ $\frac{26}{28}$

Adding Fractions with Like Denominators

	When adding fractions with like denominators:	
$\frac{2}{5}$ + $\frac{1}{5}$ / $\frac{3}{5}$	1. Add the numerators. 2. Keep the same denominator. 3. Simplify if possible.	$\frac{5}{12}$ + $\frac{5}{12}$ / $\frac{10}{12} = \frac{5}{6}$

Add. Simplify if possible.

1.
$\frac{3}{5}$
$+\ \frac{1}{5}$

$\frac{1}{3}$
$+\ \frac{1}{3}$

$\frac{1}{6}$
$+\ \frac{3}{6}$

2.
$\frac{1}{7}$
$+\ \frac{2}{7}$

$\frac{1}{4}$
$+\ \frac{1}{4}$

$\frac{1}{12}$
$+\ \frac{4}{12}$

3.
$\frac{3}{6}$
$+\ \frac{2}{6}$

$\frac{1}{11}$
$+\ \frac{3}{11}$

$\frac{3}{8}$
$+\ \frac{3}{8}$

4.
$\frac{2}{9}$
$+\ \frac{2}{9}$

$\frac{3}{12}$
$+\ \frac{5}{12}$

$\frac{5}{11}$
$+\ \frac{2}{11}$

Adding Fractions

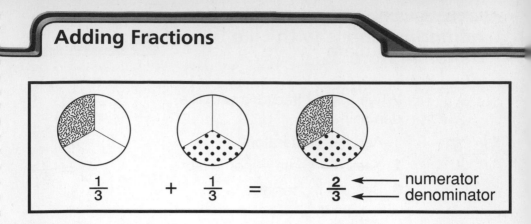

$$\frac{1}{3} \quad + \quad \frac{1}{3} \quad = \quad \frac{2}{3}$$ ← numerator
← denominator

Fill in the blanks and color in the blank objects using the information given.

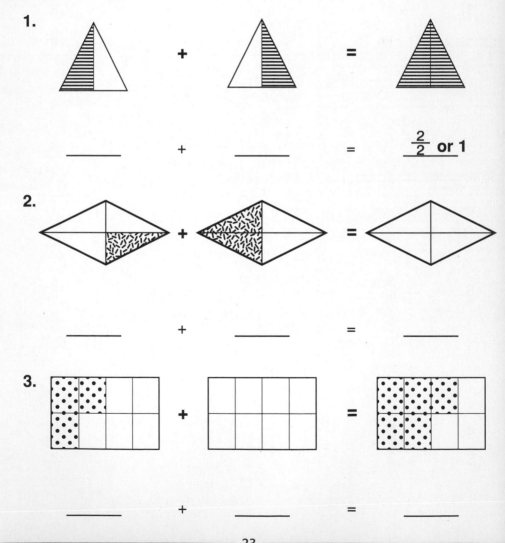

1.

_____ + _____ = $\frac{2}{2}$ **or 1**

2.

_____ + _____ = _____

3.

_____ + _____ = _____

Subtracting Fractions from a Whole Number

To subtract a fraction from a whole number:

1. Rewrite the whole number as a mixed number with an equivalent fraction using the LCD.

2. Subtract.

$$3 \longrightarrow 2\tfrac{4}{4}$$
$$-\tfrac{1}{4} \longrightarrow \tfrac{1}{4}$$
$$2\tfrac{3}{4}$$

Subtract.

1.

$$5$$
$$-\tfrac{7}{8}$$

$$3$$
$$-\tfrac{1}{3}$$

$$6$$
$$-\tfrac{7}{9}$$

2.

$$8$$
$$-\tfrac{4}{5}$$

$$5$$
$$-\tfrac{4}{9}$$

$$12$$
$$-\tfrac{3}{11}$$

3.

$$7$$
$$-\tfrac{1}{3}$$

$$10$$
$$-\tfrac{1}{5}$$

$$12$$
$$-\tfrac{7}{10}$$

Rewrite $3\frac{1}{4}$ so you can subtract.

$3\frac{1}{4} = 2 + 1\frac{1}{4} = 2\frac{5}{4}$

$-1\frac{3}{4} \longrightarrow 1\frac{3}{4}$

$1\frac{2}{4} = 1\frac{1}{2}$

Rewrite $6\frac{2}{9}$ so you can subtract.

$6\frac{2}{9} = 5 + 1\frac{2}{9} = 5\frac{11}{9}$

$-5\frac{4}{9} \longrightarrow 5\frac{4}{9}$

$\frac{7}{9}$

Subtract. Simplify if possible.

1.

$3\frac{3}{7}$
$-1\frac{5}{7}$

$5\frac{1}{3}$
$-2\frac{2}{3}$

$4\frac{1}{6}$
$-3\frac{5}{6}$

2.

$6\frac{1}{5}$
$-3\frac{3}{5}$

$4\frac{3}{10}$
$-3\frac{7}{10}$

$8\frac{2}{5}$
$-5\frac{4}{5}$

3.

$3\frac{1}{8}$
$-2\frac{5}{8}$

$6\frac{4}{9}$
$-5\frac{7}{9}$

$12\frac{5}{12}$
$-10\frac{7}{12}$

Subtracting Fractions with Unlike Denominators

To subtract fractions with unlike denominators:

1. Find the LCD.

2. Rewrite using LCD.

3. Subtract.

$$\frac{2}{5} \rightarrow \frac{2 \times 3}{5 \times 3} \rightarrow \frac{6}{15}$$

$$-\frac{1}{3} \rightarrow \frac{1 \times 5}{3 \times 5} \rightarrow \frac{5}{15}$$

$$\frac{1}{15}$$

Subtract. Simplify if possible.

1.
$$\frac{2}{3}$$
$$-\frac{1}{4}$$

$$\frac{4}{5}$$
$$-\frac{1}{2}$$

$$\frac{1}{2}$$
$$-\frac{1}{3}$$

2.
$$\frac{1}{2}$$
$$-\frac{2}{9}$$

$$\frac{2}{3}$$
$$-\frac{2}{7}$$

$$\frac{3}{4}$$
$$-\frac{1}{5}$$

3.
$$\frac{3}{5}$$
$$-\frac{2}{9}$$

$$\frac{7}{8}$$
$$-\frac{2}{5}$$

$$\frac{5}{6}$$
$$-\frac{1}{7}$$

Subtracting Mixed Numbers with Unlike Denominators

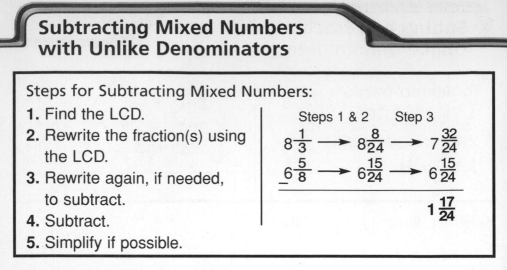

Steps for Subtracting Mixed Numbers:

1. Find the LCD.
2. Rewrite the fraction(s) using the LCD.
3. Rewrite again, if needed, to subtract.
4. Subtract.
5. Simplify if possible.

Steps 1 & 2   Step 3

$$8\tfrac{1}{3} \longrightarrow 8\tfrac{8}{24} \longrightarrow 7\tfrac{32}{24}$$
$$\underline{6\tfrac{5}{8}} \longrightarrow \underline{6\tfrac{15}{24}} \longrightarrow \underline{6\tfrac{15}{24}}$$
$$1\tfrac{17}{24}$$

Subtract. Simplify if possible.

1. $4\tfrac{1}{3}$ $6\tfrac{1}{8}$ $5\tfrac{1}{4}$
    $-\,2\tfrac{1}{2}$ $-\,5\tfrac{1}{6}$ $-\,3\tfrac{1}{2}$

2. $6\tfrac{3}{8}$ $4\tfrac{2}{9}$ $9\tfrac{1}{6}$
    $-\,5\tfrac{3}{4}$ $-\,3\tfrac{2}{3}$ $-\,7\tfrac{1}{3}$

3. $6\tfrac{1}{3}$ $7\tfrac{1}{4}$ $9\tfrac{3}{10}$
    $-\,4\tfrac{5}{8}$ $-\,3\tfrac{7}{8}$ $-\,5\tfrac{4}{5}$

Adding & Subtracting Fractions Review

To add or subtract fractions when the denominators are the same, just add or subtract the numerators. The denominators don't change. Try to picture each problem in your head.

$$\frac{2}{3} + \frac{2}{3} = \frac{4}{3}$$

or $1\frac{1}{3}$

Add or subtract. Rewrite improper fractions as mixed numbers.

1. $\frac{2}{6}$
    $-\frac{1}{6}$

2. $\frac{3}{4}$
    $+\frac{1}{4}$

3. $\frac{6}{8}$
    $-\frac{5}{8}$

4. $\frac{4}{5}$
    $+\frac{1}{5}$

5. $\frac{7}{8}$
    $+\frac{4}{8}$

6. $\frac{9}{11}$
    $+\frac{2}{11}$

7. $\frac{3}{10}$
    $+\frac{3}{10}$

8. $\frac{4}{9}$
    $+\frac{6}{9}$

9. $\frac{8}{12}$
    $-\frac{2}{12}$

Adding & Subtracting Mixed Numbers with Like Denominators

To add or subtract mixed numbers whose fractions have the same denominator:

Step 1	**Step 2**	**Step 3**
Add or subtract the numerators of the fraction part.	Add or subtract the whole numbers.	Simplify.

$$
\begin{array}{r}
2\frac{7}{9} \\
+\,4\frac{8}{9} \\
\hline
\frac{15}{9}
\end{array}
\qquad
\begin{array}{r}
\mathbf{2\frac{7}{9}} \\
\mathbf{+\,4\frac{8}{9}} \\
\hline
\mathbf{6\frac{15}{9}}
\end{array}
\qquad
\begin{array}{r}
2\frac{7}{9} \\
+\,4\frac{8}{9} \\
\hline
6\frac{15}{9} = \\
7\frac{6}{9}\ \text{or}\ \mathbf{7\frac{2}{3}}
\end{array}
$$

Write each sum or difference in simplest form.

1.
$$
\begin{array}{r}
3\frac{1}{3} \\
+\,1\frac{2}{3} \\
\hline
\end{array}
\qquad
\begin{array}{r}
6\frac{7}{10} \\
-\,2\frac{3}{10} \\
\hline
\end{array}
\qquad
\begin{array}{r}
4\frac{5}{6} \\
-\,\frac{1}{6} \\
\hline
\end{array}
$$

2.
$$
\begin{array}{r}
4\frac{1}{2} \\
+\,4\frac{1}{2} \\
\hline
\end{array}
\qquad
\begin{array}{r}
5\frac{2}{3} \\
-\,4 \\
\hline
\end{array}
\qquad
\begin{array}{r}
3\frac{1}{2} \\
-\,1\frac{1}{2} \\
\hline
\end{array}
$$

3.
$$
\begin{array}{r}
7\frac{3}{8} \\
-\,5 \\
\hline
\end{array}
\qquad
\begin{array}{r}
6\frac{3}{4} \\
+\,\frac{3}{4} \\
\hline
\end{array}
\qquad
\begin{array}{r}
5\frac{11}{14} \\
-\,2\frac{3}{14} \\
\hline
\end{array}
$$

34

Adding & Subtracting Fractions with Unlike Denominators

Write equivalent fractions with the lowest common denominator. Then add or subtract the numerator. Simplify your answer.

$$\frac{5}{6} = \frac{10}{12}$$
$$+ \frac{3}{4} = +\frac{9}{12}$$
$$\frac{19}{12} = 1\frac{7}{12}$$

Add or subtract. Write the answer in simplest form.

1.
$$\frac{2}{3}$$
$$+ \frac{1}{4}$$

$$\frac{5}{6}$$
$$- \frac{4}{9}$$

$$\frac{2}{5}$$
$$+ \frac{7}{10}$$

2.
$$\frac{3}{8}$$
$$+ \frac{5}{6}$$

$$\frac{1}{2}$$
$$+ \frac{7}{8}$$

$$\frac{2}{3}$$
$$- \frac{3}{5}$$

3.
$$\frac{1}{2}$$
$$- \frac{3}{10}$$

$$\frac{1}{2}$$
$$+ \frac{4}{5}$$

$$\frac{3}{10}$$
$$- \frac{1}{6}$$

4.
$$\frac{1}{6}$$
$$- \frac{1}{12}$$

$$\frac{2}{15}$$
$$+ \frac{1}{6}$$

It's like adding apples and oranges!

Adding & Subtracting Mixed Numbers with Unlike Denominators

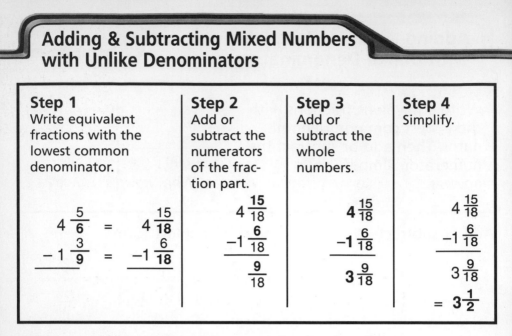

Step 1
Write equivalent fractions with the lowest common denominator.

$$4\frac{5}{6} = 4\frac{15}{18}$$
$$-1\frac{3}{9} = -1\frac{6}{18}$$

Step 2
Add or subtract the numerators of the fraction part.

$$\begin{array}{r} 4\frac{15}{18} \\ -1\frac{6}{18} \\ \hline \frac{9}{18} \end{array}$$

Step 3
Add or subtract the whole numbers.

$$\begin{array}{r} 4\frac{15}{18} \\ -1\frac{6}{18} \\ \hline 3\frac{9}{18} \end{array}$$

Step 4
Simplify.

$$\begin{array}{r} 4\frac{15}{18} \\ -1\frac{6}{18} \\ \hline 3\frac{9}{18} \end{array}$$
$$= 3\frac{1}{2}$$

Add or subtract. Write the answer in simplest form.

1.
$$\begin{array}{r} 4\frac{1}{10} \\ +\,3\frac{1}{2} \\ \hline \end{array}$$

$$\begin{array}{r} 7\frac{5}{4} \\ +\,5\frac{1}{6} \\ \hline \end{array}$$

$$\begin{array}{r} 6\frac{7}{8} \\ +\,2\frac{3}{4} \\ \hline \end{array}$$

2.
$$\begin{array}{r} 12\frac{7}{8} \\ -\,6\frac{1}{3} \\ \hline \end{array}$$

$$\begin{array}{r} 36\frac{1}{2} \\ -\,25\frac{3}{10} \\ \hline \end{array}$$

$$\begin{array}{r} 15\frac{5}{9} \\ -\,9\frac{1}{3} \\ \hline \end{array}$$

3.
$$\begin{array}{r} 12\frac{7}{8} \\ +\,6\frac{1}{3} \\ \hline \end{array}$$

$$\begin{array}{r} 9\frac{7}{8} \\ +\,4\frac{5}{6} \\ \hline \end{array}$$

$$\begin{array}{r} 8\frac{1}{10} \\ +\,5\frac{1}{4} \\ \hline \end{array}$$

Problem Solving

Solve each problem.
Write answers in simplest terms.

1. An extra-large pepperoni pizza was cut into 16 equal slices. A total of 10 slices of pizza were eaten. What fraction of the pizza was left over?

2. Four friends shared a pizza. Maria ate $\frac{1}{3}$ of the pizza, Ally and Mindy each ate $\frac{1}{4}$ of the pizza, and Bethany ate $\frac{1}{6}$.

   a. Into how many equal slices did they need to cut the pizza?

   b. How many slices of pizza did each girl eat?

3. In a survey on vegetable toppings, $\frac{3}{4}$ of the sixth-grade students said they liked green peppers on their pizza, $\frac{5}{8}$ said they liked mushrooms, and $\frac{2}{3}$ of the students said they liked onions. (Some students liked more than one choice.)

   a. Which of the three choices do more of the students like?

   b. Which of the three choices do the least number of students like?

4. Each medium pizza weighs 54 ounces. The pizza dough alone weighs 21 ounces. What fraction of the pizza's weight is the pizza dough?

Problem Solving: Fractions in a Bar Graph

The Chamber of Commerce surveyed tourists to see what activities they participated in while visiting the capital city. The graph shows the fraction of all tourists who took part in each activity.

Solve using the graph. Write all fractions in simplest form.

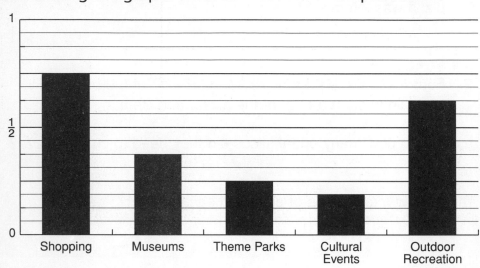

1. Which activities were chosen by more than $\frac{1}{2}$ of the tourists?

2. What fraction of tourists participated in the least popular activity?

3. What fraction of the tourists participated in the most popular activity?

4. Which activity did $\frac{5}{8}$ of the tourists participate in?

5. What fraction of the tourists visited theme parks?

Problem Solving

Leave answers as fractions. Simplify if possible.

Jobs	Tanya's Time per Job	Tyrell's Time per Job
Homework	$2\frac{1}{4}$ hours	$1\frac{2}{3}$ hours
Clean bathroom	$\frac{3}{4}$ hour	$\frac{1}{2}$ hour
Clean bedroom	$\frac{1}{3}$ hour	1 hour
Walk dog	$\frac{1}{2}$ hour	$\frac{3}{4}$ hour

1. How much total time does it take Tanya and Tyrell to do their homework?

2. How much more time does Tanya spend on her homework than Tyrell?

3. How much more time does Tyrell spend cleaning his bedroom than Tanya?

4. If Tyrell comes home from school, does his homework, and then walks the dog, how much time will it take him?

5. If Tanya cleans only once a week, how much time does she spend cleaning the bathroom and bedroom per week?

6. If Tyrell cleans the bathroom two times a week, and Tanya cleans the bathroom only once a week, who spends more time cleaning the bathroom?

Addition & Subtraction Practice with Magic Squares

When you add the numbers in each row, column, and diagonal of a magic square, the sums are the same. Find the missing numbers in each magic square below. The magic sums are given.

$\frac{4}{15}$		$\frac{8}{15}$
	$\frac{1}{3}$	
$\frac{2}{15}$		$\frac{2}{5}$

The magic sum is 1.

$1\frac{4}{5}$		$2\frac{3}{5}$
	$1\frac{1}{2}$	
	$2\frac{9}{10}$	$1\frac{1}{5}$

The magic sum is $4\frac{1}{2}$.

$1\frac{1}{8}$		$1\frac{3}{8}$
$1\frac{1}{4}$		$1\frac{1}{2}$

The magic sum is $3\frac{15}{16}$.

$2\frac{1}{3}$		$2\frac{4}{9}$
$2\frac{1}{9}$		$2\frac{2}{9}$

The magic sum is $6\frac{5}{6}$.

40

©RBP Books

Probability

Probability is the chance of an event occurring. The probability of an event can be described as **likely, unlikely, certain,** or **impossible.**

Suppose we fill up a sack with 10 marbles.
One is green and 9 are red.

The probability of pulling out a green marble is **unlikely**.

The probability of pulling out a red marble is **likely**.

The probability of pulling out a yellow marble is **impossible**.

The probability of pulling out a green or red marble is **certain**.

Look at the spinner to answer the following questions. Circle the best answer.

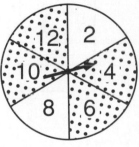

1. The probability of spinning an even number is
   likely   unlikely   certain   impossible

2. The probability of spinning a odd number is
   likely   unlikely   certain   impossible

3. The probability of landing on a polka-dotted space is
   likely   unlikely   certain   impossible

4. The probability of landing on a number greater than 8 is
   likely   unlikely   certain   impossible

5. The probability of landing on a 2 is
   likely   unlikely   certain   impossible

Probability

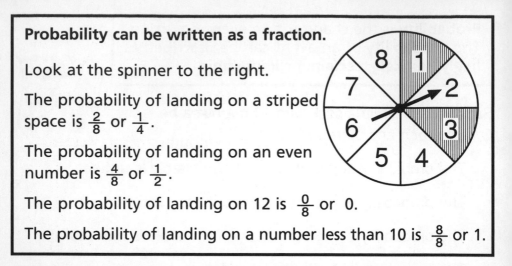

Probability can be written as a fraction.

Look at the spinner to the right.

The probability of landing on a striped space is $\frac{2}{8}$ or $\frac{1}{4}$.

The probability of landing on an even number is $\frac{4}{8}$ or $\frac{1}{2}$.

The probability of landing on 12 is $\frac{0}{8}$ or 0.

The probability of landing on a number less than 10 is $\frac{8}{8}$ or 1.

Imagine if we turned over the cards below, mixed them up, and then picked one card. Answer the following questions by writing a fraction.

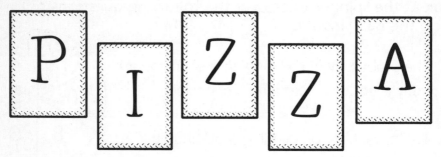

1. What is the probability of picking a P?

2. What is the probability of picking a Z?

3. What is the probability of picking an E?

4. What is the probability of picking a number?

5. What is the probability of picking any letter?

6. What is the probability of picking a vowel?

Probability

Maria's mother keeps a box full of mismatched socks. In the box there are 5 white, 4 blue, 1 red, 1 gray, and 3 black socks.

What is the probability of pulling out a blue sock?

The probability would equal the number of blue socks over the total number of socks.

$$\frac{\text{Blue}}{\text{Total}} = \frac{4}{5 + 4 + 1 + 1 + 3} = \frac{4}{14} = \frac{2}{7}$$

Holly bought a box of candy that had the following colors: 14 brown, 8 yellow, 2 blue, and 6 red. Without looking she pulled out one candy.

1. What is the probability that it is yellow?

2. What is the probability that it is red?

3. What is the probability that it is purple?

4. What is the probability that it is brown?

Raymond has a fruit basket on the kitchen table. It contains 4 green apples, 5 red apples, and 6 oranges. He grabs one piece of fruit.

5. What is the probability that it is red?

6. What is the probability that it is a fruit?

7. What is the probability that it is an orange?

8. What is the probability that it is an apple?

Fractions, Decimals, Percents—RBP0822

Multiplying Fractions

$\frac{1}{2} \times \frac{1}{4}$ can be visualized as:

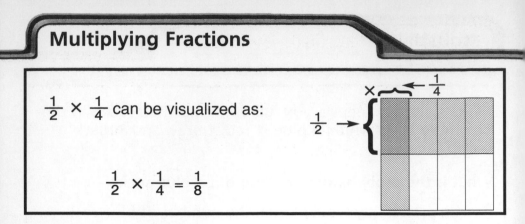

$$\frac{1}{2} \times \frac{1}{4} = \frac{1}{8}$$

Use the grids to multiply fractions.

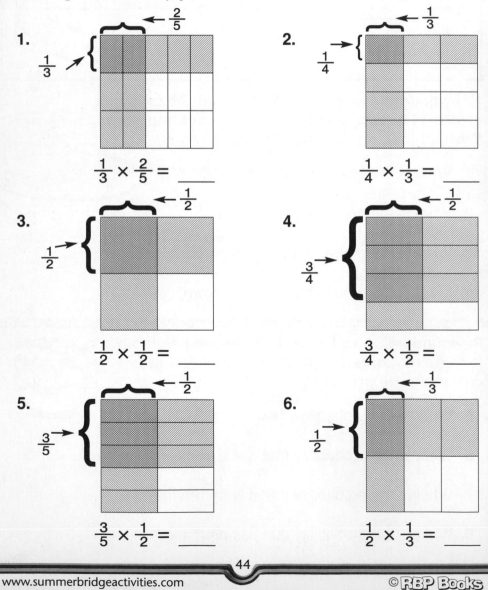

1.

$$\frac{1}{3} \times \frac{2}{5} = \underline{\hspace{1cm}}$$

2.

$$\frac{1}{4} \times \frac{1}{3} = \underline{\hspace{1cm}}$$

3.

$$\frac{1}{2} \times \frac{1}{2} = \underline{\hspace{1cm}}$$

4.

$$\frac{3}{4} \times \frac{1}{2} = \underline{\hspace{1cm}}$$

5.

$$\frac{3}{5} \times \frac{1}{2} = \underline{\hspace{1cm}}$$

6.

$$\frac{1}{2} \times \frac{1}{3} = \underline{\hspace{1cm}}$$

www.summerbridgeactivities.com

Multiplying Fractions by Whole Numbers

When multiplying a whole number and a fraction:

1. Rewrite the whole number as a fraction (write a denominator of 1).
2. Multiply the numerators.
3. Multiply the denominators.
4. Simplify if possible.

$$\frac{3}{4} \times 6 = \frac{3}{4} \times \frac{6}{1}$$
$$= \frac{3 \times 6}{4 \times 1}$$
$$= \frac{18}{4}$$
$$= 4\frac{2}{4} = 4\frac{1}{2}$$

Multiply. Simplify if possible.

1. $3 \times \frac{2}{3} =$ $\frac{4}{5} \times 2 =$ $1 \times \frac{6}{7} =$

2. $\frac{2}{5} \times 6 =$ $3 \times \frac{3}{10} =$ $9 \times \frac{3}{4} =$

3. $8 \times \frac{1}{6} =$ $2 \times \frac{6}{7} =$ $6 \times \frac{1}{10} =$

4. $\frac{3}{10} \times 5 =$ $5 \times \frac{2}{9} =$ $\frac{3}{7} \times 2 =$

Multiplying Mixed Numbers by Fractions

When multiplying a mixed number and a fraction:

1. Rewrite the mixed number as an improper fraction.
2. Multiply the numerators.
3. Multiply the denominators.
4. Simplify if possible.

$$2\frac{1}{3} \times \frac{4}{5} = \frac{7}{3} \times \frac{4}{5}$$
$$= \frac{7 \times 4}{3 \times 5}$$
$$= \frac{28}{15}$$
$$= 1\frac{13}{15}$$

Multiply. Simplify if possible.

1. $\frac{1}{2} \times 1\frac{1}{8} =$ $\qquad$ $2\frac{1}{3} \times \frac{1}{3} =$ $\qquad$ $4\frac{1}{2} \times \frac{1}{3} =$

2. $3\frac{1}{2} \times \frac{1}{4} =$ $\qquad$ $\frac{3}{5} \times 3\frac{1}{2} =$ $\qquad$ $\frac{2}{5} \times 3\frac{1}{3} =$

3. $4\frac{3}{4} \times \frac{1}{3} =$ $\qquad$ $\frac{1}{9} \times 2\frac{1}{2} =$ $\qquad$ $\frac{1}{2} \times 1\frac{3}{5} =$

4. $4\frac{2}{3} \times \frac{3}{4} =$ $\qquad$ $9\frac{1}{2} \times \frac{1}{6} =$ $\qquad$ $3\frac{3}{4} \times \frac{5}{12} =$

Multiplying Fractions

Multiply. Simplify if possible.

1. $\frac{3}{4} \times \frac{1}{2} =$ $\frac{1}{3} \times \frac{2}{5} =$ $\frac{4}{5} \times \frac{1}{3} =$

2. $\frac{2}{3} \times \frac{3}{5} =$ $\frac{4}{5} \times \frac{5}{9} =$ $\frac{3}{8} \times \frac{4}{5} =$

3. $6 \times \frac{1}{3} =$ $5 \times \frac{1}{2} =$ $\frac{2}{3} \times 8 =$

4. $\frac{2}{3} \times 1\frac{1}{2} =$ $1\frac{4}{5} \times \frac{1}{3} =$ $2\frac{1}{4} \times \frac{1}{3} =$

5. $2\frac{3}{4} \times 5 =$ $2 \times 1\frac{1}{2} =$

Whoa!
I'm
multiplying!

Problem Solving

1. Austin is going to the movie theater. It is $3\frac{3}{5}$ miles from his house. Austin decides to take his electric scooter, but it breaks down $\frac{2}{3}$ of the way to the theater. How far is Austin from his house?

2. Austin's electric scooter uses $\frac{1}{4}$ gallon of fuel each mile. How much fuel has he used since he left home?

   (Hint: Use your answer from question 1.)

3. Austin purchases $\frac{2}{3}$ pound of Yum-Yum Treats. If Yum-Yum Treats are $6.00 per pound, how much does Austin pay?

4. In the theater, Austin meets 2 of his friends, who have bought 1 gigantic barrel of popcorn. Only $\frac{3}{4}$ of it is left. Austin eats $\frac{1}{3}$ of what is left. How much of the barrel does Austin eat?

Converting Fractions into Percents

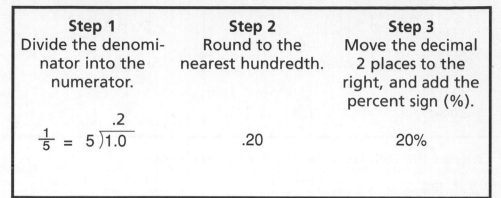

Step 1	Step 2	Step 3
Divide the denominator into the numerator.	Round to the nearest hundredth.	Move the decimal 2 places to the right, and add the percent sign (%).

$$\frac{1}{5} = 5\overline{)1.0}^{\;.2}$$

.20

20%

Convert the following fractions into percents.

1. $\frac{3}{8}$

2. $\frac{1}{3}$

3. $\frac{4}{7}$

4. $\frac{1}{4}$

5. $\frac{2}{3}$

6. $\frac{1}{10}$

7. $\frac{2}{5}$

8. $\frac{9}{20}$

9. $\frac{3}{4}$

10. $\frac{1}{2}$

Converting Percents into Fractions

Step 1	Step 2
Step 1	**Step 2**
Put the percent over 100.	Simplify.
20% $\frac{20}{100}$	$\frac{1}{5}$

Convert the following percents into fractions.

1. 5%

2. 23%

3. 10%

4. 50%

5. 75%

6. 2%

7. 40%

8. 100%

Rounding Decimal Numbers

Round each number to the nearest tenth.

1. 4.58 _____   **2.** 19.96 _____   **3.** 8.16 _____

12.87 _____   20.08 _____   9.42 _____

Round each number to the nearest hundredth.

4. 6.877 _____   **5.** 4.058 _____   **6.** 97.470 _____

8.876 _____   87.069 _____   1.387 _____

Round each number to the nearest thousandth.

7. 1.0649 _____   **8.** 93.0129 _____   **9.** 7.2199 _____

22.5240 _____   51.8490 _____   3.7672 _____

Comparing Decimals

Comparing decimals is similar to comparing whole numbers.

Example .08 ◯ .8

1. Line up the numbers by place value.

   .08
   .8

2. Compare the digits left to right. After the decimal point, you have a 0 and an 8. The 8 is bigger than 0, so .8 is greater than .08.

   .08 (<) .8

Put the correct sign (>, <, =) in each problem.

1. .007 ◯ .07

2. 2.159 ◯ 2.259

3. 10.05 ◯ 10.005

4. 0.99 ◯ .009

5. 30.249 ◯ 30.429

6. .004 ◯ 4.00

7. 6.041 ◯ 6.401

8. 92.001 ◯ 92.001

9. 263.08 ◯ 263.81

10. .08 ◯ .8

11. 101.05 ◯ 101.005

12. 9.50 ◯ 7.05

13. 214.01 ◯ 214.001

14. 9.008 ◯ 9.08

Menu Mix-up

Put the prices on the menu in order from least to greatest.

$1.25 $2.03 $1.07 $2.51 $1.10 $2.15 $2.21 $1.05

Item:	Price:
Soda	
Milk	
Fries	
Salad	
Cheese Sandwich	
Tuna Sandwich	
Hamburger	
Cheeseburger	

Circle the largest decimal number in each row.

1.   4.05   4.50   4.005   4.15   4.55   4.5

2.   10.57   10.49   10.005   10.057   10.75   10.094

3.   2.5   2.15   2.52   2.005   2.095   2.51

4.   1.8   1.84   1.48   1.847   1.75   1.5

Fractions, Decimals, Percents—RBP0822

Adding Decimals

When adding decimals, line up the decimal points.

$$3.5 + 1.06 + .45 =$$

Add each column.

$$\begin{array}{r} 1\,1 \\ 3.5 \\ 1.06 \\ +\ .45 \\ \hline 5.01 \end{array}$$

Bring the decimal point straight down.

Add the numbers below. Don't forget the decimal point in your answer.

1. 3.63 + 4.8 =

2. 95.02 + 1.15 =

3. 17.7 + 5.2 =

4. 4.83 + 7.8 + 6.9 =

5. 7.30 + 15.81 + 11 =

6.
$$\begin{array}{r} 37.5 \\ 9.26 \\ +\ \ \ .07 \\ \hline \end{array}$$

7.
$$\begin{array}{r} 4.2 \\ 85.37 \\ +\ 11 \\ \hline \end{array}$$

8.
$$\begin{array}{r} 12.7 \\ 286 \\ +\ \ \ \ .03 \\ \hline \end{array}$$

9. 5.74 + 8.7 + 9.6 =

10. 7.30 + 15.81 + 6.4 =

Subtracting Decimals

When subtracting decimals, line up the
decimal points.

		$\overset{3}{\cancel{4}}\overset{1}{}$
5.4	5.40	5.40
− .17	− .17	− .17
		5.23

Subtract the decimals below.
Place a zero to fill empty spaces as needed.

1.   2.6
       − 1.8

2.   23.1
       − .05

3.   6.7
       − 1.6

4. 82.3
      − 1.54

5. $5.4 - 2.1 =$

6. $6.58 - 3.2 =$

7. $41 - 2.6 =$

8. $17.8 - .56 =$

9. $7.5 - .64 =$

10. $13.9 - 1.25 =$

11.   10.4
       − 2.43

12.   3.77
       − 1.2

13.   17.8
       − 11.0

Multiplying Numbers with Decimals

Step 1	Step 2	Step 3
Multiply.	Count the number of places (from right to left) over to the decimal point on both numbers.	Place the decimal point in the answer by starting at the right and moving the point the number of spaces you counted.

Step 1
.41
x 8.9
369
3280
3649

Step 2
.41
.9
3 places

Step 3
.41
x 8.9
369
3280
3.649

Multiply the following:

1. 5.6
x 8

2. .045
x 6

3. 6.21
x 7

4. 62.6
x 5

5. 2.26
x 3

6. 31.2
x 48

7. .725
x 54

8. 66.1
x 5.7

9. 67.2
x .28

10. .532
x .64

11. .3 x 4.61 =

12. .32 x .81 =

13. 2.51 x 40 =

Dividing Numbers with Decimals

Step 1	Step 2	Additional Step
Divide.	Place the decimal point in the answer as shown below.	Add zeros if needed.

Step 1 — Divide.

$$.06\overline{)\,.084} \quad \begin{array}{r} 14 \\ \hline 6 \\ 24 \\ 24 \\ \hline 0 \end{array}$$

Step 2 — Place the decimal point in the answer as shown below.

$$.06\overline{)\,.084} = 1.4$$

Additional Step — Add zeros if needed.

$$5\overline{)\,28} \quad \begin{array}{r} 5 \\ \hline 25 \\ 3 \end{array} \qquad 5\overline{)\,28.0} \quad \begin{array}{r} 5.6 \\ \hline 25 \\ 3\,0 \end{array}$$

Divide the following:

1. $4\overline{)\,.166}$ **2.** $.4\overline{)\,.48}$ **3.** $.6\overline{)\,1.8}$ **4.** $5\overline{)\,.95}$

5. $7\overline{)\,7.14}$ **6.** $.6\overline{)\,.198}$ **7.** $.9\overline{)\,42.3}$ **8.** $.6\overline{)\,48.90}$

9. $4\overline{)\,3.62}$ **10.** $50\overline{)\,7.25}$ **11.** $25\overline{)\,2.26}$ **12.** $.03\overline{)\,.0009}$

© RBP Books   Fractions, Decimals, Percents—RBP0822

Converting Fractions into Decimals

Step 1	Step 2
Divide the denominator into the numerator. Add zeros if necessary.	Round to the nearest hundredth.

$\frac{1}{3} = \quad 3\,\overline{)1.000}$

$$\begin{array}{r} .333 \\ 3\,\overline{)1.000} \\ \underline{-9} \\ 10 \\ \underline{-9} \\ 1\text{(etc.)} \end{array}$$

Round .333 to .33.

Convert the following into decimals:

1. $\frac{3}{4}$ 2. $\frac{7}{12}$ 3. $\frac{1}{10}$ 4. $\frac{2}{5}$

5. $\frac{3}{2}$ 6. $\frac{1}{6}$ 7. $\frac{2}{3}$ 8. $\frac{1}{4}$

9. $\frac{5}{4}$ 10. $\frac{4}{5}$ 11. $\frac{1}{5}$ 12. $\frac{3}{8}$

13. $\frac{7}{10}$ 14. $\frac{50}{100}$ 15. $\frac{1}{2}$

Multiplying Decimal Numbers

Solve each problem.

Remember to write the decimal point in your answer.

1.
$$\begin{array}{r} {}^{5\ 3}2.64 \\ \times\ \ 9 \\ \hline \mathbf{23.76} \end{array}$$

2.
$$\begin{array}{r} 6.48 \\ \times\ \ 7 \\ \hline \end{array}$$

3.
$$\begin{array}{r} 72.7 \\ \times\ \ 8 \\ \hline \end{array}$$

4.
$$\begin{array}{r} 12.9 \\ \times\ \ 17 \\ \hline \end{array}$$

5.
$$\begin{array}{r} 54.87 \\ \times\ \ 24 \\ \hline \end{array}$$

6.
$$\begin{array}{r} 97.02 \\ \times\ \ 32 \\ \hline \end{array}$$

7.
$$\begin{array}{r} 3.348 \\ \times\ \ 63 \\ \hline \end{array}$$

8.
$$\begin{array}{r} 4.05 \\ \times\ \ 69 \\ \hline \end{array}$$

9.
$$\begin{array}{r} 2.469 \\ \times\ 236 \\ \hline \end{array}$$

10.
$$\begin{array}{r} 6.009 \\ \times\ \ 48 \\ \hline \end{array}$$

11.
$$\begin{array}{r} 71.865 \\ \times\ \ 45 \\ \hline \end{array}$$

12.
$$\begin{array}{r} 98.077 \\ \times\ \ 45 \\ \hline \end{array}$$

Fractions, Decimals, Percents—RBP0822

Which Costs More?

Use the price list to solve each problem.

Remember to write the decimal point in your answer.

Item	Price per Pound
apples	$0.97
bananas	$0.56
peaches	$0.72
pears	$0.84
plums	$0.65
oranges	$0.33
grapes	$1.09

1. Anne buys 3 pounds of bananas. Meg buys 5 pounds of apples. Who spends more, Anne or Meg?

2. James buys 6 pounds of peaches. How much does James spend on peaches?

3. If Susan buys 4 pounds of oranges and 3 pounds of pears, which fruit does she spend the most money on, oranges or pears?

4. Mason buys 9 pounds of grapes. His sister buys 10 pounds of apples. Who spends more, Mason or his sister?

5. Travis buys 7 pounds of pears. Lisa buys 8 pounds of peaches. Who spends more, Travis or Lisa?

6. Jesse buys 5 pounds of oranges and 4 pounds of bananas. What does she spend the most money on, oranges or bananas?

©RBP Books

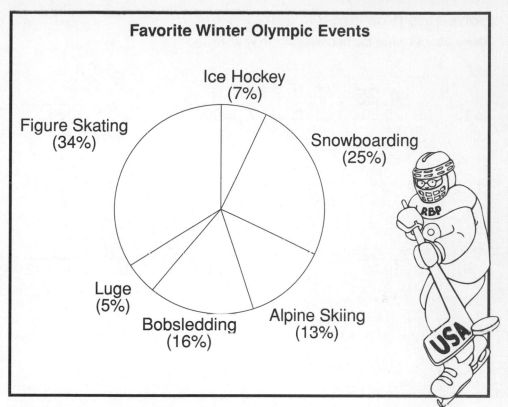

Favorite Winter Olympic Events

Ice Hockey (7%)

Snowboarding (25%)

Figure Skating (34%)

Luge (5%)

Bobsledding (16%)

Alpine Skiing (13%)

Megan's class voted on their favorite Winter Olympic events. Use the circle graph to answer the questions.

1. Which event received the highest number of votes?

2. What percent of students voted for bobsledding?

3. Which event did 34% of the students vote for as their favorite?

4. What was the total percentage of students who liked the luge and bobsledding altogether?

5. How many more students voted for snowboarding than alpine skiing?

On-the-Dot Division: Dividing Decimals

Solve each problem.

Remember to write the decimal point in your answer.

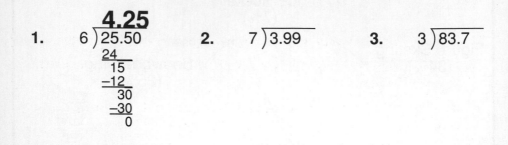

1.
$$\begin{array}{r} 4.25 \\ 6\overline{)25.50} \\ \underline{24} \\ 15 \\ \underline{-12} \\ 30 \\ \underline{-30} \\ 0 \end{array}$$

2. $7\overline{)3.99}$

3. $3\overline{)83.7}$

4. $3\overline{)19.05}$

5. $7\overline{)11.62}$

6. $4\overline{)49.12}$

7. $8\overline{)1.96}$

8. $7\overline{)55.86}$

9. $2\overline{)12.62}$

10. $4\overline{)3.04}$

11. $2\overline{)1.826}$

12. $9\overline{)5.526}$

Remember... Probability is the chance or possibility that an event will happen.

The probability of something happening can be written as a fraction.

$\dfrac{3}{12}$ The **numerator** tells the number of chances for a specific event.

The **denominator** tells the total number of possible things that could happen.

- If the fraction that describes the probability is equal to 1, the event is **certain**.
- If the fraction is greater than another, the event is **more likely**.
- If the fraction is less than another, the event is **less likely**.
- If the fraction that describes the probability is 0, the event is **impossible**.

Find the probability. Write it as a fraction.

Penny has 11 pencils in her pencil box. Two pencils are orange, 3 pencils are blue, 5 pencils are yellow, and 1 pencil is green.

1.
What is the probability that Penny will pull out an **orange** pencil?

2.
What is the probability that Penny will pull out a **green** pencil?

3.
What is the probability that Penny will pull out a **blue** pencil?

4.
What is the probability that Penny will pull out a **black** pencil?

5.
What is the probability that Penny will pull out a **yellow** pencil?

6.
What color pencil is Penny **most likely** to pull out of her pencil box?

73

Notes

_____
_____
_____
_____
_____
_____
_____
_____
_____
_____
_____
_____
_____
_____
_____
_____
_____
_____
_____
_____
_____
_____
_____
_____

5 Five things I'm thankful for:

1. _____
2. _____
3. _____
4. _____
5. _____

Answer Pages

Page 3

1. $\frac{5}{6}$ 2. $\frac{1}{8}$ 3. $\frac{2}{3}$
4. $\frac{4}{8}$ 5. $\frac{16}{32}$ 6. $\frac{3}{12}$

Page 4

1.

2.

3.

4.

5.

Page 5

1. $\frac{3}{5}$; $\frac{3}{4}$ 2. $\frac{4}{9}$; $\frac{1}{4}$
3. $\frac{1}{3}$; $\frac{6}{12}$ 4. $\frac{2}{8}$; $\frac{4}{10}$
5. $\frac{4}{5}$; $\frac{5}{11}$ 6. $\frac{1}{2}$; $\frac{7}{8}$
7. one-third   two-thirds
8. one-half   one-eighth
9. three-eighths   four-elevenths
10. two-fifths   five-thirds
11. five-sevenths   five-ninths

Page 6

1. $\frac{3}{8}$ $\frac{5}{8}$; $\frac{4}{6}$ $\frac{2}{6}$; $\frac{4}{8}$ $\frac{4}{8}$
2. $\frac{1}{4}$ $\frac{3}{4}$; $\frac{2}{3}$ $\frac{1}{3}$; $\frac{1}{8}$ $\frac{7}{8}$
3. $\frac{1}{2}$ $\frac{1}{2}$; $\frac{1}{3}$ $\frac{2}{3}$; $\frac{2}{3}$ $\frac{1}{3}$
4. $\frac{3}{6}$ $\frac{3}{6}$; $\frac{1}{6}$ $\frac{5}{6}$; $\frac{2}{6}$ $\frac{4}{6}$

Page 7

1. >   2. >   3. >
4. >   5. <   6. >
7. <   8. =   9. =
10. <   11. <   12. =

Page 8

1. $\frac{2}{2}$, 1   2. $\frac{11}{6}$, $1\frac{5}{6}$ 3. $\frac{6}{5}$, $1\frac{1}{5}$
4. $\frac{7}{3}$, $2\frac{1}{3}$ 5. $\frac{11}{4}$, $2\frac{3}{4}$ 6. $\frac{17}{6}$, $2\frac{5}{6}$

Page 9

1. $1\frac{1}{4}$ 2. $3\frac{1}{3}$ 3. $1\frac{1}{8}$
4. $2\frac{1}{2}$ 5. $1\frac{3}{4}$ 6. 3
7. $1\frac{3}{7}$ 8. $2\frac{3}{8}$ 9. $1\frac{4}{5}$
10. $2\frac{3}{10}$ 11. $2\frac{1}{8}$ 12. $4\frac{1}{3}$
13. $3\frac{1}{9}$ 14. $2\frac{1}{4}$ 15. $2\frac{1}{6}$

Page 10

1. $7\frac{1}{2}$ $1\frac{3}{4}$ $2\frac{6}{7}$
2. $8\frac{3}{5}$ $2\frac{7}{8}$ $4\frac{1}{5}$
3. $2\frac{7}{12}$ $2\frac{1}{2}$ $1\frac{5}{8}$
4. $2\frac{3}{4}$ $5\frac{4}{9}$ $6\frac{5}{6}$

Page 11

1. $\frac{7}{3}$ $\frac{27}{4}$ $\frac{13}{12}$
2. $\frac{25}{8}$ $\frac{38}{5}$ $\frac{19}{10}$
3. $\frac{17}{5}$ $\frac{103}{11}$ $\frac{27}{7}$
4. $\frac{29}{5}$ $\frac{53}{12}$ $\frac{73}{11}$

Page 12

1. $\frac{1}{2}$ $\frac{2}{5}$ $\frac{1}{3}$
2. $\frac{2}{3}$ $\frac{1}{3}$ $\frac{3}{5}$
3. $\frac{3}{4}$ $\frac{1}{12}$ $\frac{2}{3}$
4. $\frac{1}{3}$ $\frac{1}{4}$ $\frac{5}{6}$

Page 13

1. $2\frac{1}{2}$ $3\frac{1}{3}$ $2\frac{3}{4}$
2. $1\frac{2}{3}$ $6\frac{1}{2}$ 7
3. $2\frac{1}{4}$ $4\frac{1}{3}$ $6\frac{1}{2}$
4.   7 $5\frac{1}{4}$ $3\frac{1}{2}$

Fractions, Decimals, Percents—RBP0822

Answer Pages

Page 14
1. $\frac{1}{3}$ $\frac{2}{3}$ $\frac{5}{6}$
2. $\frac{3}{4}$ $\frac{1}{6}$ $\frac{1}{2}$
3. $1\frac{1}{8}$ $2\frac{1}{5}$ $2\frac{2}{3}$
4. $5\frac{1}{3}$ $1\frac{1}{2}$ $4\frac{1}{2}$
5. $1\frac{1}{3}$ $2\frac{2}{3}$ $4\frac{1}{4}$

Page 15
1. 9 12 4
2. 4 15 12
3. 15 4 10

Page 16
1. $\frac{1}{3}=\frac{2}{6}\ \frac{3}{9}\ \cancel{\frac{4}{8}}\ \frac{5}{15}$
2. $\frac{1}{4}=\frac{2}{8}\ \cancel{\frac{3}{6}}\ \frac{4}{16}\ \frac{5}{20}$
3. $\frac{1}{5}=\cancel{\frac{2}{6}}\ \frac{2}{10}\ \frac{3}{15}\ \frac{4}{20}$
4. $\frac{2}{3}=\frac{4}{6}\ \frac{6}{9}\ \cancel{\frac{8}{16}}\ \frac{10}{15}$
5. $\frac{3}{12}$ 6. $\frac{2}{3}$ 7. $\frac{10}{16}$
8. $\frac{9}{12}$ 9. $\frac{1}{6}$ 10. $\frac{6}{9}$

Page 17
1. 6: 1, 2, 3, 6   4: 1, 2, 4
   18: 1, 2, 3, 6, 9, 18   12: 1, 2, 3, 4, 6, 12
   GCF: 6   GCF: 4
2. 12: 1, 2, 3, 4, 6, 12   14: 1, 2, 7, 14
   18: 1, 2, 3, 6, 9, 18   21: 1, 3, 7, 21
   GCF: 6   GCF: 7
3. 18: 1, 2, 3, 6, 9, 18   24: 1, 2, 3, 4, 6, 8, 12, 24
   27: 1, 3, 9, 27   32: 1, 2, 4, 8, 16, 32
   GCF: 9   GCF: 8
4. 9: 1, 3, 9   9: 1, 3, 9
   12: 1, 2, 3, 4, 6, 12   15: 1, 3, 5, 15
   GCF: 3   GCF: 3
5. 15: 1, 3, 5, 15   15: 1, 3, 5, 15
   20: 1, 2, 4, 5, 10, 20   40: 1, 2, 4, 5, 8, 10, 20, 40
   GCF: 5   GCF: 5

Page 18
1. $\frac{2}{3}$ $\frac{1}{2}$ $\frac{3}{5}$
2. $\frac{1}{9}$ $\frac{5}{18}$ $\frac{5}{6}$
3. $\frac{2}{7}$ $\frac{2}{3}$ $\frac{11}{15}$
4. $\frac{1}{3}$ $\frac{1}{2}$ $\frac{4}{5}$
5. $\frac{34}{59}$ $\frac{1}{4}$ $\frac{13}{14}$

Page 19
1. 6: 6, 12, 18, 24   4: 4, 8, 12, 16, 20
   2: 2, 4, 6, 8, 10   8: 8, 16, 24, 32
   LCM: 6   LCM: 8
2. 5: 5, 10, 15, 20   4: 4, 8, 12, 16
   3: 3, 6, 9, 12, 15, 18   6: 6, 12, 18, 24
   LCM: 15   LCM: 12
3. 8: 8, 16, 24, 32, 40   6: 6, 12, 18, 24, 30
   12: 12, 24, 36, 48   10: 10, 20, 30, 40, 50
   LCM: 24   LCM: 30
4. 12: 12, 24, 36, 48, 60   10: 10, 20, 30, 40, 50
   20: 20, 40, 60, 80   15: 15, 30, 45, 60
   LCM: 60   LCM: 30
5. 8: 8, 16, 24, 32, 40   4: 4, 8, 12, 16, 20, 24, 28, 32, 36
   10: 10, 20, 30, 40, 50   18: 18, 36, 54, 72
   LCM: 40   LCM: 36

Page 20
1. $\frac{1}{9},\frac{3}{9}$ $\frac{2}{6},\frac{1}{6}$
2. $\frac{12}{24},\frac{16}{24}$ $\frac{6}{18},\frac{6}{18}$
3. $\frac{14}{28},\frac{12}{28}$ $\frac{16}{24},\frac{18}{24}$
4. $\frac{2}{16},\frac{1}{16}$ $\frac{1}{12},\frac{3}{12}$
5. $\frac{12}{18},\frac{3}{18}$ $\frac{8}{32},\frac{4}{32}$

Page 21
1. = > >
2. > < >
3. < > =
4. $\frac{1}{3},\frac{7}{12},\frac{5}{6}$ $\frac{3}{4},\frac{13}{16},\frac{7}{8}$
5. $\frac{1}{2},\frac{3}{4},\frac{5}{6}$ $\frac{3}{8},\frac{3}{7},\frac{3}{5}$

Page 22
1. 2   2. $\frac{1}{4}$ cup
3. $2\frac{1}{2}$ teaspoons   4. $7\frac{1}{2}$ cups
5. $2\frac{1}{2}$ cups   6. coconut

Page 23
1. $\frac{1}{2};\frac{1}{2}$ 2. $\frac{1}{4};\frac{2}{4};\frac{3}{4}$ 3. $\frac{3}{8};\frac{2}{8};\frac{5}{8}$

Page 24
1. $\frac{4}{5}$ $\frac{2}{3}$ $\frac{2}{3}$
2. $\frac{3}{7}$ $\frac{1}{2}$ $\frac{5}{12}$
3. $\frac{5}{6}$ $\frac{4}{11}$ $\frac{3}{4}$
4. $\frac{4}{9}$ $\frac{2}{3}$ $\frac{7}{11}$

Answer Pages

Page 25
1. $5\frac{2}{3}$ $4\frac{3}{5}$ 6
2. $6\frac{1}{5}$ $14\frac{1}{2}$ $4\frac{1}{2}$
3. 13 $6\frac{1}{3}$ $4\frac{1}{10}$
4. $5\frac{3}{4}$ $8\frac{1}{3}$ $18\frac{1}{3}$

Page 26
1. $\frac{11}{15}$ $\frac{17}{24}$ $\frac{5}{6}$
2. $1\frac{7}{30}$ $\frac{20}{21}$ $\frac{19}{30}$
3. $\frac{25}{28}$ $\frac{23}{24}$ $1\frac{1}{12}$

Page 27
1. $5\frac{13}{24}$ $5\frac{19}{20}$ $7\frac{1}{6}$
2. $7\frac{1}{4}$ $7\frac{11}{16}$ $6\frac{11}{12}$
3. $7\frac{1}{4}$ $5\frac{1}{10}$ $9\frac{7}{8}$

Page 28
1. $\frac{1}{4}$ $\frac{1}{6}$ $\frac{2}{3}$
2. $\frac{5}{6}$ $\frac{3}{5}$ $\frac{2}{5}$
3. $\frac{1}{2}$ $\frac{1}{2}$ $\frac{7}{11}$

Page 29
1. $4\frac{1}{8}$ $2\frac{2}{3}$ $5\frac{2}{9}$
2. $7\frac{1}{5}$ $4\frac{5}{9}$ $11\frac{8}{11}$
3. $6\frac{2}{3}$ $9\frac{4}{5}$ $11\frac{3}{10}$

Page 30
1. $1\frac{5}{7}$ $2\frac{2}{3}$ $\frac{1}{3}$
2. $2\frac{3}{5}$ $\frac{3}{5}$ $2\frac{3}{5}$
3. $\frac{1}{2}$ $\frac{2}{3}$ $1\frac{5}{6}$

Page 31
1. $\frac{5}{12}$ $\frac{3}{10}$ $\frac{1}{6}$
2. $\frac{5}{18}$ $\frac{8}{21}$ $\frac{11}{20}$
3. $\frac{17}{45}$ $\frac{19}{40}$ $\frac{29}{42}$

Page 32
1. $1\frac{5}{6}$ $\frac{23}{24}$ $1\frac{3}{4}$
2. $\frac{5}{8}$ $\frac{5}{9}$ $1\frac{5}{6}$
3. $1\frac{17}{24}$ $3\frac{3}{8}$ $3\frac{1}{2}$

Page 33
1. $\frac{1}{6}$ 2. 1   3. $\frac{1}{8}$
4. 1   5. $1\frac{3}{8}$ 6. 1
7. $\frac{3}{5}$ 8. $1\frac{1}{9}$ 9. $\frac{1}{2}$

Page 34
1. 5 $4\frac{2}{5}$ $4\frac{2}{3}$
2. 9 $1\frac{2}{3}$ 2
3. $2\frac{3}{8}$ $7\frac{1}{2}$ $3\frac{4}{7}$

Page 35
1. $\frac{11}{12}$ $\frac{7}{18}$ $1\frac{1}{10}$
2. $1\frac{5}{24}$ $1\frac{3}{8}$ $\frac{1}{15}$
3. $\frac{1}{5}$ $1\frac{3}{10}$ $\frac{2}{15}$
4. $\frac{1}{12}$ $\frac{3}{10}$

Page 36
1. $7\frac{3}{5}$ $13\frac{5}{12}$ $9\frac{5}{8}$
2. $6\frac{13}{24}$ $11\frac{1}{5}$ $6\frac{2}{9}$
3. $19\frac{5}{24}$ $14\frac{17}{24}$ $13\frac{7}{20}$

Page 37
1. $\frac{6}{16}$ or $\frac{3}{8}$ of the pizza
2. **a.** 12 slices
   b. Maria = 4 slices, Ally = 3 slices, Mindy = 3 slices, Bethany = 2 slices
3. **a.** green peppers **b.** mushrooms
4. $\frac{21}{54}$ or $\frac{7}{18}$

Page 38
1. Shopping, Outdoor Recreation
2. $\frac{3}{16}$ Cultural Events
3. $\frac{3}{4}$ Shopping
4. Outdoor Recreation
5. $\frac{1}{4}$

Page 39
1. $3\frac{11}{12}$ hours   2. $\frac{7}{12}$ hour
3. $\frac{2}{3}$ hour   4. $2\frac{5}{12}$ hours
5. $1\frac{1}{12}$ hours   6. Tyrell

Fractions, Decimals, Percents—RBP0822

Answer Pages

Page 40

1. $\frac{1}{5}$ $\frac{3}{5}$ $\frac{1}{15}$ $\frac{7}{15}$
2. $\frac{1}{10}$ 2 $\frac{3}{10}$ $\frac{7}{10}$ $\frac{2}{5}$
3. $1\frac{7}{16}$ $1\frac{9}{16}$ $1\frac{5}{16}$ $1\frac{1}{16}$ $1\frac{3}{16}$
4. $2\frac{1}{18}$ $2\frac{7}{18}$ $2\frac{5}{18}$ $2\frac{1}{6}$ $2\frac{1}{2}$

Page 41

1. certain
2. impossible
3. likely
4. unlikely
5. unlikely

Page 42

1. $\frac{1}{5}$ 2. $\frac{2}{5}$ 3. 0
4. 0   5. 1   6. $\frac{2}{5}$

Page 43

1. $\frac{4}{15}$ 2. $\frac{1}{5}$ 3. 0   4. $\frac{7}{15}$
5. $\frac{1}{3}$ 6. 1   7. $\frac{2}{5}$ 8. $\frac{3}{5}$

Page 44

1. $\frac{2}{15}$ 2. $\frac{1}{12}$ 3. $\frac{1}{4}$ 4. $\frac{3}{8}$
5. $\frac{3}{10}$ 6. $\frac{1}{6}$

Page 45

1.   2 $1\frac{3}{5}$ $\frac{6}{7}$
2. $2\frac{2}{5}$ $\frac{9}{10}$ $6\frac{3}{4}$
3. $1\frac{1}{3}$ $1\frac{5}{7}$ $\frac{3}{5}$
4. $1\frac{1}{2}$ $1\frac{1}{9}$ $\frac{6}{7}$

Page 46

1. $\frac{9}{16}$ $\frac{7}{9}$ $1\frac{1}{2}$
2. $\frac{7}{8}$ $2\frac{1}{10}$ $1\frac{1}{3}$
3. $1\frac{7}{12}$ $\frac{5}{18}$ $\frac{4}{5}$
4. $3\frac{1}{2}$ $1\frac{7}{12}$ $1\frac{9}{16}$

Page 47

1. $\frac{3}{8}$ $\frac{2}{15}$ $\frac{4}{15}$
2. $\frac{2}{5}$ $\frac{4}{9}$ $\frac{3}{10}$
3.   2 $2\frac{1}{2}$ $5\frac{1}{3}$
4.   1 $\frac{3}{5}$ $\frac{3}{4}$
5. $13\frac{3}{4}$ 3

Page 48

1. $2\frac{2}{5}$ miles   2. $\frac{3}{5}$ gallon
3. $4.00   4. $\frac{1}{4}$ barrel

Page 49

1. 3 students   2. 9 girls
3. 4 students   4. $\frac{3}{4}$ hour

Page 50

1. $\frac{3}{10}$
2. one and twelve-hundredths; $1\frac{12}{100}$
3. .221; $\frac{221}{1000}$
4. .53; fifty-three hundredths
5. eight hundred seventy-one thousandths; $\frac{871}{1000}$

Page 51

1. $\frac{2}{10}$; .2   2. $\frac{8}{10}$; .8
3. $\frac{9}{10}$; .9   4. $\frac{1}{10}$; .1
5. $\frac{13}{100}$; .13   6. $\frac{87}{100}$; .87

Page 52

1. $\frac{25}{100}$ or $\frac{1}{4}$ 2. $\frac{2}{100}$ or $\frac{1}{50}$
3. $\frac{120}{100}$ or $1\frac{1}{5}$ 4. $\frac{40}{100}$ or $\frac{2}{5}$
5. $\frac{15}{100}$ or $\frac{3}{20}$ 6. $\frac{58}{100}$ or $\frac{29}{50}$
7. $\frac{510}{100}$ or $5\frac{1}{10}$ 8. $\frac{80}{100}$ or $\frac{4}{5}$

Page 53

1. 38%   2. 33%   3. 57%   4. 25%
5. 67%   6. 10%   7. 40%   8. 45%
9. 75%   10. 50%

Page 54

1. $\frac{5}{100}$ or $\frac{1}{20}$ 2. $\frac{23}{100}$
3. $\frac{10}{100}$ or $\frac{1}{10}$ 4. $\frac{50}{100}$ or $\frac{1}{2}$
5. $\frac{75}{100}$ or $\frac{3}{4}$ 6. $\frac{2}{100}$ or $\frac{1}{50}$
7. $\frac{40}{100}$ or $\frac{2}{5}$ 8. $\frac{100}{100}$ or 1

78

Answer Pages

Page 55
1. .90
2. .40
3. .051
4. .10
5. .75
6. .25
7. .546
8. .06
9. .15
10. .489
11. .08
12. .23
13. .18
14. .515
15. .09
16. .99
17. .054
18. 1

Page 56
1. $\frac{5}{100}$ .05 5%
2. $\frac{14}{100}$ .14 14%
3. $\frac{27}{100}$ .27 27%
4. $\frac{32}{100}$ .32 32%
5. $\frac{89}{100}$ .89 89%
6. $\frac{57}{100}$ .57 57%
7. $\frac{9}{100}$ .09 9
8. $\frac{17}{100}$ .17 17%
9. $\frac{71}{100}$ .71 71%
10. $\frac{43}{100}$ .43 43%
11. $\frac{34}{100}$ .34 34%
12. $\frac{64}{100}$ .64 64%
13. $\frac{75}{100}$ .75 75%

Page 57
1. .05
2. .007
3. .92
4. .084
5. .07
6. .043
7. .7
8. .15
9. .9
10. $\frac{75}{100}$
11. $\frac{3}{100}$
12. $\frac{86}{1000}$
13. $\frac{21}{1000}$
14. $\frac{4}{100}$
15. $\frac{21}{100}$
16. $\frac{9}{100}$
17. $\frac{11}{100}$
18. $\frac{5}{1000}$
19. 8%
20. 19%
21. 21%
22. 72%
23. 33%
24. 98%
25. 62%
26. 7%
27. 4%

Page 58
1. .04
2. .006
3. .036
4. .10
5. .027
6. .92
7. .047
8. .89
9. .2
10. .08

Page 59
1. 3.6
2. 1.08
3. 7.2
4. 4.002
5. 6.01
6. 8.02
7. 3.032
8. 9.7
9. 108.7
10. 34.04
11. 56.93
12. 20.09
13. 64.02
14. 216.3
15. 81.5
16. 42.009
17. 82.05
18. 16.7
19. 38.5
20. 11.27

Page 60
1. 2.1 5.4 7.4 26.6
2. 5.7 33.0 69 122.2
3. 7.4 8.6 5 80.8
4. 3.05 62.69 1.59 51.97
5. 9.92 4.77 5.82 81.75
6. 8.04 27.98 3.25 6.38

Page 61
1. 4.6 12.9
2. 20.0 20.1
3. 8.2 9.4
4. 6.88 8.88
5. 4.06 87.07
6. 97.47 1.39
7. 1.065 22.524
8. 93.013 51.849
9. 7.220 3.767

Page 62
1. <
2. <
3. >
4. >
5. <
6. <
7. <
8. =
9. <
10. <
11. >
12. >
13. >
14. <

Page 63
Soda $1.05; Milk $1.07; Fries $1.10;
Salad $1.25; Cheese Sandwich $2.03;
Tuna Sandwich $2.15; Hamburger $2.21;
Cheeseburger $2.51
1. 4.55
2. 10.75
3. 2.52
4. 1.847

Page 64
1. 8.43
2. 96.17
3. 22.9
4. 19.53
5. 34.11
6. 46.83
7. 100.57
8. 298.73
9. 24.04
10. 29.51

Page 65
1. .8
2. 23.05
3. 5.1
4. 80.76
5. 3.3
6. 3.38
7. 38.4
8. 17.24
9. 6.86
10. 12.65
11. 7.97
12. 2.57
13. 6.8

Page 66
1. 44.8
2. .27
3. 43.47
4. 313
5. 6.78
6. 1,497.6
7. 39.15
8. 376.77
9. 18.816
10. .34048
11. 1.383
12. .2592
13. 100.4

Answer Pages

Page 67
1. .0415	**2.** 1.2	**3.** 3
4. .19	**5.** 1.02	**6.** .33
7. 47	**8.** 81.5	**9.** .905
10. .145	**11.** .0904	**12.** .03

Page 68
1. .75	**2.** .58	**3.** .10
4. .40	**5.** 1.50	**6.** .17
7. .67	**8.** .25	**9.** 1.25
10. .80	**11.** .20	**12.** .38
13. .70	**14.** .50	**15.** .50

Page 69
1. 23.76	**2.** 45.36	**3.** 581.6
4. 219.3	**5.** 1,316.88	**6.** 3,104.64
7. 210.924	**8.** 279.45	**9.** 582.684
10. 288.432	**11.** 3,233.925	
12. 4,413.465		

Page 70
1. Meg	**2.** $4.32	**3.** pears
4. Mason	**5.** Travis	**6.** bananas

Page 71
1. figure skating	**2.** 16%
3. figure skating	**4.** 21%
5. 12%	

Page 72
1. 4.25	**2.** .57	**3.** 27.9
4. 6.35	**5.** 1.66	**6.** 12.28
7. .245	**8.** 7.98	**9.** 6.31
10. .76	**11.** .913	**12.** .614

Page 73
1. $\frac{2}{11}$

2. $\frac{1}{11}$

3. $\frac{3}{11}$

4. 0

5. $\frac{5}{11}$

6. yellow